VOCABULARY NINJA WORKBOOK

ANDREW JENNINGS

Contents

3......Introduction

Level 1 Grasshopper

4......Object Elaboration
5......Dark, Easy, New, Old
6......Vocabulary Builder
7......**Topic Focus** –
         Ancient Greece

Level 2 Shinobi

8......Expanded Elaboration
9......Verb Victory
10....Adverb Antics
11....**Topic Focus** –
         Food Chains and Habitats

Level 3 Warrior

12....Coordinating Conjunctions
13....Adventurous Alternatives
14....Sorting Synonyms
15....Colour Connections
16....**Topic Focus** – Queen Victoria

Level 4 Samurai

17....'Said' Words
18....Crossword Conundrum
19....Word Wizardry
20....Word Jumble
21....**Topic Focus** – Marvellous Mountains

Level 5 Assassin

22....It's All Relative... Pronouns
23....Varying 'Very'
24....Subordinating Conjunctions
25....Alphabet Action
26....**Topic Focus** – Vikings

Level 6 Grand Master

27....Personification Powers
28....Alphabet A-Z
29....Developing Detail
30....Secret Ninja Vocabulary
31....**Topic Focus** – Natural Disasters

32....**Answers**

BLOOMSBURY EDUCATION
LONDON   OXFORD   NEW YORK   NEW DELHI   SYDNEY

BLOOMSBURY EDUCATION
Bloomsbury Publishing Plc
50 Bedford Square, London, WC1B 3DP, UK
29 Earlsfort Terrace, Dublin 2, Ireland

BLOOMSBURY, BLOOMSBURY EDUCATION and the Diana logo are trademarks of Bloomsbury Publishing Plc
First published in Great Britain 2021 by Bloomsbury Publishing Plc
Text copyright © Andrew Jennings, 2021
Ninja illustrations copyright © Andrew Jennings, 2021
All other illustrations © Shutterstock, 2021

Andrew Jennings has asserted his right under the Copyright, Designs and Patents Act, 1988,
to be identified as Author of this work

Bloomsbury Publishing Plc does not have any control over, or responsibility for, any third-party websites referred to or in this book. All internet addresses given in this book were correct at the time of going to press. The author and publisher regret any inconvenience caused if addresses have changed or sites have ceased to exist, but can accept no responsibility for any such changes

All rights reserved. No part of this publication may be reproduced or transmitted in any form or by any means, electronic or mechanical, including photocopying, recording, or any information storage or retrieval system, without prior permission in writing from the publishers

A catalogue record for this book is available from the British Library

ISBN: PB: 978-1-4729-8099-1; ePDF: 978-1-4729-8089-2

2 4 6 8 10 9 7 5 3 1 (paperback)

Text design by Jeni Child

Printed and bound in China by Leo Paper Products, Heshan, Guangdong

MIX
Paper from responsible sources
FSC® C020056

All papers used by Bloomsbury Publishing Plc are natural, recyclable products from wood grown in well managed forests and other sources. The manufacturing processes conform to the environmental regulations of the country of origin

To find out more about our authors and books visit www.bloomsbury.com and sign up for our newsletters

Introduction

When we think about being successful in education and life, we naturally think of the importance of reading and writing, but not so much vocabulary. Interestingly, in maths a child's understanding of their times tables is seen as crucial, as they are the foundations of any further mathematical activity a child does in school and beyond. Well, vocabulary is just as crucial. Not just for reading and writing, but for the whole curriculum as well as your child's wider understanding of the world around them, how it works and how they communicate with it. Vocabulary, or words, underpins all forms of knowledge acquisition and communication development. Words will literally unlock the doors to a world of understanding for your child.

Vocabulary Ninja Workbooks provide a comprehensive introduction to vocabulary, focusing on a variety of areas to enhance your child's curriculum knowledge and develop their reading and writing skills. The range of exciting activities, games and challenges include:

World of Words

A range of activities designed to develop an understanding of the world, focusing specifically on objects and emotions.

Curriculum Topic Vocabulary

Specially-selected vocabulary from key National Curriculum topics covered in each year group to help develop your child's subject-specific vocabulary.

Breadth and Depth Activities

Activities that introduce new and exciting vocabulary, with the primary focus of widening your child's vocabulary and deepening their understanding.

Grammar-Focused Activities

Activities that support the development of grammar and the vocabulary associated with it, in line with the curriculum requirements for grammar.

Vocabulary Laboratory

Games, challenges and puzzles are littered throughout the book, providing engaging and exciting ways for your child to recall and use the vocabulary they have learnt.

Creative Writing

Vocabulary for creative writing is built up throughout the book, starting with a focus on interesting descriptive words and increasing in complexity until finishing with writing activities that enable your child to apply the vocabulary from the earlier stages.

Ninja Tip

Discussing, using and playing with the vocabulary from each page is just as important as getting the questions right. Where possible, try to use and model the vocabulary from the book during everyday life with your child, finding different contexts to use it in.

How to use this book

This book increases in complexity and challenge across six different sections. Your child should attempt the Grasshopper and Shinobi sections of the book as independently as possible, asking for support where necessary. As your child moves through the rest of the book, adult guidance and support is recommended to ensure your child fully understands each activity and the vocabulary in it. Don't worry though, examples are provided on most pages and answers are available at the back of the book. When your child has finished the activities, you can go to www.vocabularyninja.co.uk to download a certificate.

Level 1

Object Elaboration

'Elaborate' means to add detail. It's important to learn how to do this in your writing – it makes it more interesting.

We can elaborate on our description of an object by adding words that describe it. When doing this, think of the object's colour, size, material and smell, or even an emotion that you feel about the object.

Here are some everyday objects. Write down an interesting description of each of them. One has been done for you.

the beautiful, wooden guitar

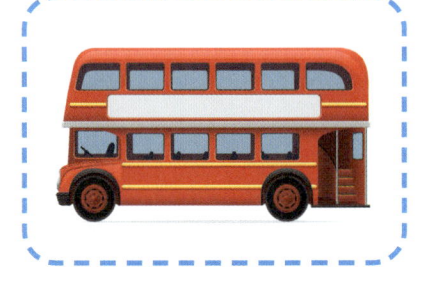

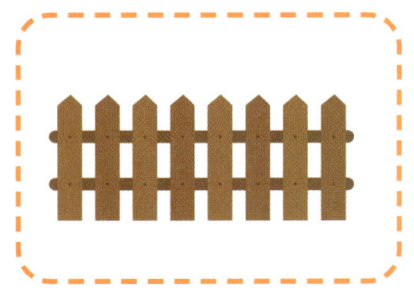

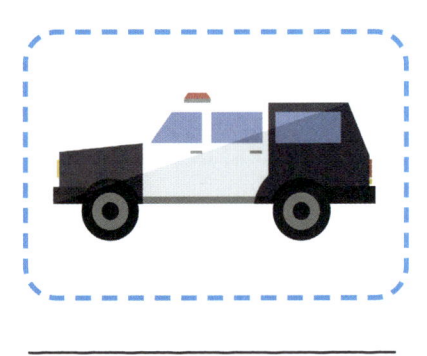

4

Dark, Easy, New, Old

Level 1

Extend your vocabulary by learning lots of different interesting words to use, instead of very common words such as happy, sad, big and small.

Circle three words in each section you can use instead of the word in colour. One has been done for you.

dark

bright (murky) nimble dusky eager obtain assist gloomy

easy

straightforward whisper leave simple effortless occupy maim

new

unused super boast fresh modern ravage perky gain

old

elderly own detest ancient tattered aged splendid travel

5

Level 1 — Vocabulary Builder

It's important to build your vocabulary word by word. These amazing words have been chosen to expand your vocabulary.

There are four common words below in colour. Each common word has lots of exciting synonyms – words that mean the same – next to it. Read all of the words, then write sentences using two of the words from each list.

Discuss the words with an adult first and develop a sentence together if you are unsure.

| beautiful | appealing | elegant | enticing | angelic | bewitching |

Example: _Their view of the sea was bewitching_____.
Sentence: _____.
Sentence: _____.

| boring | dull | repetitive | tedious | dreary | monotonous |

Sentence: _____.
Sentence: _____.

| frightened | fearful | alarmed | panicked | spooked | petrified |

Sentence: _____.
Sentence: _____.

| mysterious | strange | puzzling | curious | baffling | inexplicable |

Sentence: _____.
Sentence: _____.

Ancient Greece

Ancient Greek history has some links to things around today. One such link is the soldier whose story inspired the modern marathon race.

Fill in the gaps using the words from the Word Bank. One has been done for you.

Word Bank

Persians
defeated
warn
Spartan
~~invade~~
retreated
Marathon
Athenians
unprotected
battle
victorious

In 490 BC, a Persian army set sail to ___invade___ Greece, landing near the city of Marathon. The A_____, people from the city of Athens, used their army to block the P_____.

The Athenians sent a soldier called Pheidippedes to run to the city of Sparta to ask for the help of the S_____ army.

Back in M_____, the Athenian and Persian armies fought a b_____. The Persians were d_____ but they set sail to Athens, which was u_____ because the Athenian army was in Marathon.

Pheidippedes went to Athens to w_____ the people in the city that the Persians were coming. He also told them the Athenian army had been v_____ in the Battle of Marathon by saying 'nike', meaning 'victory'. Sadly he died after running so far. But because of his warning, the Athenian army returned from Marathon and the Persian army r_____.

Level 2

Expanded Elaboration

Make your writing more engaging for the reader by adding descriptions before an object. This is called an expanded noun phrase.

Think about the colours, shapes, emotions or verbs you could use to add interest. Some words have been added already to help you.

the ____excited____, ____joyful____ family

the _____, ____rumbling____ spaceship

the _____, _____ knight

the _____, _____ forest

the _____, _____ tablet

the _____, _____ seaside

the ____bristly____, _____ paintbrush

8

Verb Victory

Verbs tell us exactly how someone or something is behaving, moving or acting. There is a whole world of exciting verbs out there.

Fill the gaps in the sentences using the verbs from the Word Bank. One has been done for you.

Carl was careful not to _____**destroy**_____ the delicate sculpture.

_____ the bike with hot water and soap.

John needed to _____ the test, as he failed the first time.

_____ your friends to the party.

Be sure to _____ the town centre, it's too busy.

_____ for the jar on the top shelf.

Don't _____ with your sister.

You will _____ the windows with the ball.

We always used to _____ where it went.

Use the blocks to _____ a tower.

Use the stick to _____ at the clouds.

I knew she would _____ her lunch.

Word Bank

avoid
argue
build
Clean
damage
~~destroy~~
forget
Invite
point
Reach
repeat
wonder

Adverb Antics

Adverbs help us to add details to verbs. They can give detail about how, where, when, where and much more. Below are some amazing adverbs.

Use the adverbs from the Word Bank to complete the sentences below. One has been done for you.

The twins crossed the road ____safely____ by looking both ways.

_____, I ate the cake myself without sharing with anyone.

My family _____ visit the cinema, they don't like films.

Akari stomped _____ across the playground, fuming.

_____, I completed my favourite game after months of playing it.

Jim ran _____ to find his shoes.

I hid _____ Alice on the top bunk.

Mr Hussein was _____ upset after the class misbehaved.

We brushed our teeth _____ before going to bed.

The children _____ said 'Hello' to all visitors.

Word Bank

safely	above
politely	Rudely
never	quickly
carefully	Finally
very	angrily

Food Chains and Habitats

Food chains help us understand how energy is created and then moves from one living thing to another through eating. Let's look at some of the key food chain vocabulary we need to know about.

Draw lines between each label and its matching picture.
Then draw lines between each picture and the matching definition.
Some have been done for you.

Word	Picture	Definition
food chain	(seagull & fish)	eats other animals and plants for the energy provided
consumer	(fox)	a system which shows how energy is transferred from one living thing to another
producer	(badger)	an animal that is eaten by other animals
predator	(rabbit)	an animal that hunts and eats other animals
prey	(panda)	makes their own energy: this is what plants do
carnivore	(plant)	a consumer that eats plants and animals
herbivore	(man)	a consumer that eats plants
omnivore	(lion)	a consumer that eats animals

TOPIC FOCUS

11

Level 3: Coordinating Conjunctions

Conjunctions are words that allow us to join information together. Here are three coordinating conjunctions, which help us to connect two pieces of information together in slightly different ways: but, so, and.

Use the starter sentences and the conjunctions below to help you finish each sentence in different ways. Here are three examples.

Alice walked to the local shop **and** _then on to the butchers for sausages_.
Alice walked to the local shop **but** _she had forgotten her purse_.
Alice walked to the local shop **so** _she could buy milk and eggs_.

The ocean was wild **but** _____.
The ocean was wild **so** _____.
The ocean was wild **and** _____.

The leaves fell to the ground **but** _____.
The leaves fell to the ground **so** _____.
The leaves fell to the ground **and** _____.

Every day I run three miles **but** _____.
Every day I run three miles **so** _____.
Every day I run three miles **and** _____.

Adventurous Alternatives

Level 3

We tend to use quite common words, but with a bit more thought you can choose alternative words that are more creative!

There are five common words below, each accompanied by two words you can replace them with. Think of a sentence using each common word, then replace it with one of the alternative words. One has been done for you.

cute
Alternatives: delightful / enchanting
Sentence: _The kittens were cute_ _____ .
Replacement: _The kittens were enchanting_ _____

hungry
Alternatives: peckish / ravenous
Sentence: _____ _____ _____ .
Replacement: _____ _____ _____

nervous
Alternatives: anxious / tense
Sentence: _____ _____ _____ .
Replacement: _____ _____ _____

tired
Alternatives: exhausted / weepy
Sentence: _____ _____ _____ .
Replacement: _____ _____ _____

unhappy
Alternatives: despondent / miserable
Sentence: _____ _____ _____ .
Replacement: _____ _____ _____

13

Sorting Synonyms

Synonyms are words that have a very similar meaning to each other, although they sometimes vary in strength of meaning.

Use the words from the Word Bank to fill in the synonym lists. List four synonyms for each word. Two have been done for you.

strong
mighty
_____
_____
_____

cry
_____
_____
_____
_____

destroy
ravage
_____
_____
_____

Word Bank

scream	weep	wreck	annihilate
mighty	powerful	robust	ravage
whimper	sob	shatter	muscular

And the same as above, for three more target words!

interesting
_____
_____
_____
_____

loud
_____
_____
_____
_____

scared
_____
_____
_____
_____

Word Bank

gripping	fearful	compelling	alarmed
booming	deafening	absorbing	thunderous
afraid	fascinating	ear-piercing	agitated

Colour Connections

Level 3

Colours are much more to us than just red, yellow, blue and green! We can use other things from the world around us to help describe exact shades of colour.

For example, instead of just saying 'red' you could write:
After running, my cheeks were raspberry red.

Word Bank

blue	royal / sapphire	purple	lilac / violet
green	fern / emerald	yellow	mustard / butter
red	scarlet / crimson	black	ink / ebony

Choose one of each pair of replacement words from the Word Bank to fill in the gaps. One has been done for you. You don't have to use every word.

___Mustard___ yellow leaves fell gently to the ground.

Her _____ red cheeks glowed in the winter sun.

Rocks of _____ black and _____ green scattered the coast.

_____ purple blossom created a magical carpet.

The _____ blue ocean waters rose and fell gently.

The cyclist put on the _____ black gloves.

_____ green trees and _____ yellow sunlight combined to make a magical view.

_____ blue ink stained the clothing.

The _____ purple thistle stood proudly on the moor.

They rode on, as the _____ red sunset darkened.

15

Queen Victoria

Queen Victoria was one of Britain's longest serving monarchs. Let's learn more about her life as well as some words related to the time she lived in.

Fill in the gaps using the words from the Word Bank. One has been done for you.

Queen Victoria began writing a ___diary___ in 1832 and continued until her death in 1901. In total, around 44,000 pages survive. That's a lot of words! She had a wonderful v_____.

Q_____ Victoria liked photography. In 1851, Queen Victoria and Prince Albert had their collection of p_____ displayed at the Great E_____ in London. Over 6 million people came.

Sadly, Victoria's h_____ Albert died in 1861 at the age of 42. For the rest of her r_____ she wore black to m_____ his death.

The p_____ of Britain more than doubled during Queen Victoria's reign, meaning there was more d_____ for houses, food and jobs.

F_____ and m_____ were built and towns became larger, changing the l_____ and the ways people lived. R_____, originally built to t_____ goods, meant people could t_____ easily around the country for the first time.

Word Bank

Exhibition	population
husband	vocabulary
Factories	photographs
travel	landscape
demand	transport
Queen	mourn
reign	machines
~~diary~~	Railways

'Said' Words

'Said' is an awesome word as it tells us that something has been spoken. But it doesn't tell us about the way something has been spoken – the character's emotion or manner. There are many words we can use instead of 'said' to add detail.

Read the replacement words for 'said' and their definitions below. Then write sentences using each of the words. One has been done for you.

joked – spoke in a jokey way, said something funny
Sentence: *'Are you sure about that?' Tomasz joked*.

observed – spoke about something the person has seen or noticed
Sentence: _____.

sobbed – spoke while crying noisily
Sentence: _____.

barked – said orders in short aggressive bursts, like a dog barking!
Sentence: _____.

explained – said how or why something happens
Sentence: _____.

whispered – said something very quietly
Sentence: _____.

17

Crossword Conundrum

Use the clues to help you fill in the crossword using the words from the Word Bank.

You'll learn some exciting vocabulary along the way! One has been done for you.

Word Bank

tranquil   unstable   ravenous   divulge   concoct
luminous   towering   loiter   dawdle   raucous

Across

2. Waste time, be slow
4. Make, combining many ingredients
8. To tell a secret or something unknown
9. Bright and shining
10. Very tall compared to other nearby objects

Down

1. Making lots of loud noise
3. Wait around without a clear purpose
5. Calm, no noise
6. Extremely hungry
7. Likely to collapse

Word Wizardry

Level 4

Below are simple definitions of certain words. The only problem is there are four words written next to each meaning.

Use your word wizardry skills to decide which word links to each definition. Circle the correct word. One has been done for you.

★ small, tightly packed   deafening   restful   adore   (compact)

★ walk or move slowly   switch   tranquil   amble   rogue

★ lacking knowledge   ignorant   bellow   conclude   natter

★ in original condition, new   cavort   pristine   scamper   robust

★ very bad, horrible   saturate   prolong   atrocious   terminate

★ consider carefully   muscular   vivid   delay   deliberate

★ to steal   muted   pilfer   rotten   malleable

Word Jumble

Games can help us remember words.

Rearrange the letters in the mixed-up words to spell real words.
Use the clues to help you work out each jumbled word.
One has been done for you.

Jumbled word	Clue	Answer
beemd	to fix firmly in something	embed
wsamr	a large flying group of animals	_____
ceiper	go through something	_____
carne	to stretch or lean your head forward	_____
rquiev	to shiver or tremble	_____
etanmd	a bike for two people	_____
bbmoard	continuous attack using bombs	_____
agshlty	something unpleasant	_____
oomuisn	seems something unpleasant may happen	_____
asrcelt	a shade of red	_____
nnunicg	sly, able to trick people	_____

Marvellous Mountains

Level 4

Fill in the gaps using the words from each Word Bank.

Mount Everest is the _____ mountain found on Earth. Everest is _____ in the _____ in _____. Everest is around 8,848 _____ high.

Word Bank

| highest | Asia | metres | Himalayas | located |

K2 is the _____ highest mountain in the world. It is also found in the Himalayas. K2 is 8,623 metres tall and is considered _____ to _____ than Mount Everest due to its _____ weather _____.

Word Bank

| second | extreme | climb | harder | conditions |

Mount Kilimanjaro is the tallest _____ mountain in the world, at 5,895 metres, and is also a _____. Its last major _____ was around 100,000 years ago. It is made up of three volcanoes. Two are e_____, while one is d_____.

Word Bank

| free-standing | eruption | volcano | extinct | dormant |

Mont Blanc is between _____ and France and is one of the highest points in the _____. Mont Blanc is around 4,808m high, although because of the ever-changing thickness of the _____ at the _____, no _____ height is set.

Word Bank

| Alps | precise | ice | Italy | summit |

TOPIC FOCUS

It's All Relative... Pronouns

Relative pronouns may sound tricky, but they are quite the opposite. We are going to focus on three of them: who, which and that.

Relative pronouns refer back to a noun which has been mentioned earlier in a sentence. See the examples below. The relative pronouns refer back to the underlined words.

John lives in Newcastle, **which** is south of Scotland.

The player of the match was Olivia, **who** scored three goals.

I liked the round, green chair **that** was very comfortable.

Complete each sentence using the relative pronouns **who**, **which** or **that** to add more detail. One has been done for you.

I love Christmas Day _____which I always celebrate with my family_____.

My friend lives in London _____.

Pass me the red ball _____.

Fruit hung from the trees _____.

The ninja hid from her enemy _____.

The tomatoes were picked from the plant _____.

Varying 'Very'

Rather than using a mild word and making it stronger with 'very', you can just use a strong word. For example, rather than saying 'very happy', you can say 'joyful'. This is more precise and powerful writing.

Match the strong words from the Word Bank to the 'very' phrase with the same meaning. One has been done for you.

Word Bank

sluggish   vibrant   exhilarating   ~~meticulous~~   tiny
luminous   adorable   spotless   lavish   exceptional

very detailed _____meticulous_____

very colourful _____

very clean _____

very bright _____

very cute _____

very exciting _____

very fancy _____

very slow _____

very small _____

very special _____

Level 5 — Subordinating Conjunctions

Subordinating conjunctions often connect two contrasting pieces of information. Here are three subordinating conjunctions, which help us to join two pieces of information together in slightly different ways: **although, while, even though**.

Use the starter sentences and the conjunctions below to help you finish each sentence in a slightly different way. Here are three examples:

Jenny cried the deepest of blue tears, **although** _no one could see them_.
Jenny cried the deepest of blue tears, **while** _her evil smile grew wider_.
Jenny cried the deepest of blue tears, **even though** _she wasn't that upset_.

The rusty car ploughed through the snow, **although** _____.

The rusty car ploughed through the snow, **while** _____.

The rusty car ploughed through the snow, **even though** _____.

Books lined the shelves like soldiers, **although** _____.

Books lined the shelves like soldiers, **while** _____.

Books lined the shelves like soldiers, **even though** _____.

Rayyan nibbled at the crust of the sandwich, **although** _____.

Rayyan nibbled at the crust of the sandwich, **while** _____.

Rayyan nibbled at the crust of the sandwich, **even though** _____.

Alphabet Action

Let's play a game! Games help us develop and broaden our vocabularies.

Add a word that starts with the starter letter, for each of the categories. Some of the boxes have been done for you.

Letter	Fruit or vegetable	Animal	Colour	Five letter word	Adjective
A	apple	aardvark	amber	allow	afraid
B					
C			crimson		
G					
L					
M			mauve		
N			navy		
T			turquoise		
O					

You could play the game with a friend or family member. Create your own categories and starter letters and challenge them to a game!

Vikings

Level 5

The Vikings were fearsome warriors. Let's learn more about them and get to know some of the vocabulary which comes in useful when studying this topic.

Fill in the gaps in the sentences using the words from the Word Banks. One has been done for you.

Word Bank

- ~~raids~~
- Lindisfarne
- beginning
- monks
- slaves
- unarmed
- riches

Lindisfarne Raids

The Viking ____raids____ on L_____, Northumberland in 793 AD was the first serious raid on Anglo-Saxon England. This is considered the b_____ of the Viking Age. Lindisfarne was chosen because of its r_____ and the u_____, defenceless monks. Nearly all of the monks were killed in the raid, while some m_____ were taken as s_____.

Word Bank

- Heathen Army
- decades
- Norse
- raid
- Anglo-Saxon
- terrorised
- Danelaw
- Vikings

Danelaw

In the d_____ that followed, the N_____ and Danish Vikings continued to r_____ Britain, including in 865 AD when the Great H_____ A_____ landed in East Anglia. This dangerous army t_____ Anglo-Saxon England. In the 870s AD, the A_____-_____ king Alfred the Great and the Danish warlord Guthrum agreed a peace, in which they would rule different parts of England. The V_____ would rule the area of land known as the D_____.

Personification Powers

Personification is when words are used to give an object human feelings or actions.

For example: **The clouds breathed strongly on the fields below.**

Breathing is something a living creature does, not clouds. By using this word for clouds, it makes the reader imagine a strong wind, stormy clouds and plants being blown around in the fields. By using personification, you don't have to tell the reader what's happening, you can show them with imagery.

Try to create two or three examples of personification for each of the pictures below. One has been done for you.

1. The plant was crying out for water _____.
2. _____.
3. _____.

1. The sunlight danced on the waves _____.
2. _____.
3. _____.

1. _____.
2. _____.
3. _____.

1. _____.
2. _____.
3. _____.

Alphabet A-Z

Level 6

Write down as many words as you know on each line. If you can get four on each line, you will know nearly 100 words! There are a few suggestions to help you get started.

Tip – Think about all of the words you have discovered and learned from this book.

A _____ aghast _____ adorable _____
B _____
C _____ cyclone _____
D _____
E _____
F _____ forlorn _____
G _____
H _____
I _____
J _____
K _____
L _____
M _____
N _____
O _____
P _____
Q _____ quietly _____
R _____
S _____
T _____
UVW _____ Viking _____
XYZ _____

Developing Detail

Level 6

Being able to develop a detailed description makes our writing much more interesting to read – and write!

Study the picture below and note down the details you see.

Observations
What can you see in the picture? What are your first impressions?
_____
_____
_____
_____
_____

Imagery
Try to think of some powerful descriptions of the scenery.
_____
_____
_____
_____
_____

Senses
Note down a description for each of the five senses.
_____
_____
_____
_____
_____

Emotions
What might each of the people in the picture be feeling?
_____
_____
_____
_____
_____

Secret Ninja Vocabulary

Use the code matrix to discover some of Vocabulary Ninja's most powerful words.

Match the numbers in each clue to the corresponding letters to crack the code. The definitions are there to help you. One has been done already.

4	13	2	9	16	8	24	17	20	11	6	22	18
a	b	c	d	e	f	g	h	i	j	k	l	m

10	1	21	15	3	26	25	5	14	23	12	19	7
n	o	p	q	r	s	t	u	v	w	x	y	z

Clue	Definition	Answer
8, 1, 3, 22, 1, 3, 10	feel alone and unhappy	forlorn
16, 10, 25, 17, 3, 4, 22, 22, 16, 9	to be fascinated	_____
26, 25, 16, 10, 2, 17	a very bad smell	_____
22, 5, 26, 2, 20, 1, 5, 26	tastes pleasing and juicy	_____
3, 20, 9, 20, 2, 5, 22, 1, 5, 26	something to be laughed at	_____
18, 20, 26, 17, 4, 21	an accident	_____
8, 4, 9, 16	disappear bit by bit	_____
20, 10, 24, 16, 10, 20, 1, 5, 26	a very clever plan or idea	_____

30

Natural Disasters

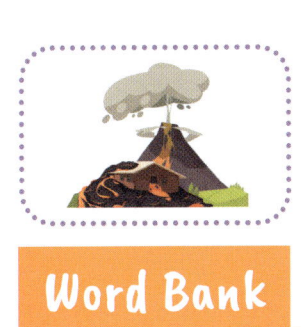

Volcanic eruption
Volcanic eruptions occur when p_____ from m_____ rock below the s_____ builds up. When volcanoes e_____ they can fire r_____ and a_____ into the air, while l_____ flows down the sides of the volcano.

Word Bank

| pressure | lava | molten | surface | erupt | rock | ash |

Hurricane
A hurricane is a huge r_____ storm of high winds which forms in w_____, t_____ conditions. Those which form in the Indian Ocean are called c_____ and those which form in East Asia are called t_____.

Word Bank

| cyclones | rotating | warm | tropical | typhoons |

Tsunami wave
Tsunamis are e_____ waves created by u_____ e_____. When the earthquakes shake the ground, enormous amounts of water are d_____, creating a huge w_____.

Word Bank

| enormous | underwater | earthquakes | wave | displaced |

Earthquake
Earthquakes occur because of t_____ p_____ moving and pushing against each other, which builds up p_____. When the pressure gets too much, lots of e_____ is released, causing the g_____ to s_____.

Word Bank

| tectonic plates | pressure | energy | shake | ground |

TOPIC FOCUS

Answers

The answers are given and pictures are numbered from left to right, top to bottom.

Level 1

Dark, Easy, New, Old
dusky, gloomy; straightforward, simple, effortless; unused, fresh, modern; elderly, ancient, aged

Ancient Greece
Athenians, Persians, Spartan, Marathon, battle, defeated, unprotected, warn, victorious, retreated

Level 2

Verb Victory
Clean, repeat, Invite, avoid, Reach, argue, damage, wonder, build, point, forget

Adverb Antics
Rudely, never, angrily, Finally, quickly, above, very, carefully, politely

Food Chains and Habitats
food chain – 1 – a system which shows how energy is transferred from one living thing to another; producer – 6 – makes their own energy: this is what plants do; predator – 2 – an animal that hunts and eats other animals; prey – 4 – an animal that is eaten by other animals; carnivore – 8 – a consumer that eats animals; herbivore – 5 – a consumer that eats plants; omnivore – 7 – a consumer that eats plants and animals

Level 3

Sorting Synonyms
powerful, robust, muscular; scream, weep, whimper, sob; wreck, annihilate, ravage, shatter

gripping, compelling, absorbing, fascinating; booming, deafening, thunderous, ear-piercing; fearful, alarmed, afraid, agitated

Colour Connections
scarlet/crimson; ink/ebony, fern/emerald; Lilac/Violet; royal/sapphire; ink/ebony; Fern/Emerald, mustard/butter; Royal/Sapphire; lilac/violet; scarlet/crimson

Queen Victoria
vocabulary, Queen, photographs, Exhibition, husband, reign, mourn, population, demand, Factories, machines, landscape, Railways, transport, travel

Level 4

Crossword Conundrum
Across: dawdle, concoct, divulge, luminous, towering
Down: raucous, loiter, ravenous, unstable

Word Wizardry
amble, ignorant, pristine, atrocious, deliberate, pilfer

Word Jumble
swarm, pierce, crane, quiver, tandem, bombard, ghastly, ominous, scarlet, cunning

Marvellous Mountains
highest, located, Himalayas, Asia, metres;
second, harder, climb, extreme, conditions;
free-standing, volcano, eruption, extinct, dormant;
Italy, Alps, ice, summit, precise

Level 5

Varying 'Very'
vibrant, spotless, luminous, adorable, exhilarating, lavish, sluggish, tiny, exceptional

Vikings
Lindisfarne, beginning, riches, unarmed, monks, slaves

decades, Norse, raid, Heathen Army, terrorised, Anglo-Saxon, Vikings, Danelaw

Level 6

Secret Ninja Vocabulary
enthralled, stench, luscious, ridiculous, mishap, fade, ingenious

Natural Disasters
pressure, molten, surface, erupt, rock, ash, lava

rotating, warm, tropical, cyclones, typhoons

enormous, underwater, earthquakes, displaced, wave

tectonic plates, pressure, energy, ground, shake